Histrionic Personality Disorder: The Ultimate Guide to Symptoms, Treatment and Prevention

By: Clayton Geoffreys

Copyright © 2015 by Clayton Geoffreys

All rights reserved. Neither this book nor any portion thereof may be reproduced or used in any manner whatsoever without the express written permission. Published in the United States of America.

Visit my website at www.claytongeoffreys.com

Cover photo by alexandria is licensed under CC BY 2.0 / modified from original

Table of Contents

Foreword 1

What is Histrionic Personality Disorder? 3

The 6 Subtypes of Histronic Personality Disorder 9

    Appeasing 9

    Tempestuous 9

    Theatrical 10

    Infantile 11

    Vivacious 12

    Disingenuous 13

What Causes Histrionic Personality Disorder? 15

The 9 Most Common Symptoms of Histrionic Personality Disorder 19

    1. Uncomfortable and/or Unhappy if Not Center of Attention 19

    2. Displays Provocative Behavior for Attention 20

3. Emotional Expressions Do Not Seem Authentic.....21

4. Utilizes Physical Appearance for Attention 22

5. Speech Patterns are Impressionistic and Lack Authenticity 22

6. Express Themselves Dramatically and Theatrically 23

7. Easily Influenced in Order to Maintain Attention on Them 24

8. See Relationships as Deeper and More Intimate Then They Actually Are 24

9. Difficulty with Maintaining Same-Sex Friendships 25

Common Therapy Methods for Histrionic Personality Disorder 27

1. Medication 27

2. Psychotherapy 30

How to Overcome Histrionic Personality Disorder 34

How to Find Your Escape 42

Conclusion 46

Final Word/About the Author 56

Endnotes 60

Disclaimer

This book is not intended as a substitute for the medical advice of a psychologist, physician, or medical professional. The reader should regularly visit a doctor or therapist in matters relating to his or her health and particularly with respect to symptoms that may require medical diagnosis or attention.

Foreword

Personality disorders can significantly alter the way one lives their life. Understanding the symptoms of these disorders is important for everyone. Whether or not you personally suffer from these disorders, learning to recognize symptoms is the first step to being able to best assist someone who may be suffering from a condition. Psychologists have studied disorders for many years, creating multiple iterations of diagnosis tools; it's difficult to truly pinpoint everything with 100% accuracy, but with time and further research, we as a society will become better aware of the nature of these disorders. Hopefully from reading *Histrionic Personality Disorder: The Ultimate Guide to Symptoms, Treatment and Prevention* I can pass along some of the abundance of information I have learned about Histrionic Personality Disorder, including its symptoms, therapies to consider, and ways to begin overcoming Histrionic disorder. Thank you for purchasing my book. Hope you enjoy and if you do, please do not forget to leave a review! Also, check out my website at claytongeoffreys.com to join my exclusive list where I let you know about my latest books. To thank you for your purchase, you can go to my site to download a free copy of <u>33 Life Lessons: Success Principles, Career Advice & Habits of Successful People</u>. In the book, you'll learn from some of the greatest thought leaders of different industries on what it takes to become successful and how to live a great life.

Cheers,

Clayton Geoffreys

What is Histrionic Personality Disorder?

Histrionic Personality Disorder is often displayed by a person who always tries to be the center of attention. Someone with Histrionic Personality Disorder will usually show extreme levels of emotion and dramatics. Many people who have this issue will also tend to use their sexuality for attention and can create problems with their own relationships and friendships. They tend to have a pack mind in a sense that they are easily influenced in order to gain the attention of others. Their dramatics make it difficult to understand their actual feelings and emotions.[1]

There are six subtypes of Histrionic Personality Disorder. Each subtype is a narrower list of portrayed social actions that confirm the diagnosis of Histrionic Personality Disorder. The symptoms span around the central goal of attention reception for the patient.

Utilizing different exaggerations of emotion and their own flamboyance, they are able to gain a crowd or to have people dote on them. The actual source of the disorder is really unknown. There are ideas that it can be genetic, but most analysis has led to the belief that it is either a coping mechanism or learned behavior. The only treatments that are available are medication for underlying issues and psychotherapy to try to sort out a specific source and how the person transforms their needs into behavior. One of the more effective ways to deal with a personality problem is through meditation and learning to escape in order to find moments of peace.

Histrionic Personality Disorder has six different subtypes. **Appeasing** subtypes function on a need to satisfy and help everyone. They become consumed in the acts of helping and doing everything for other people. **Tempestuous** subtypes have a very moody and brooding disposition. **Theatrical** subtypes are considered the purest type as it involves the most exact symptoms of Histrionic Personality Disorder. They are very theatrical and overly falsified. Usually everything they do is over the top and obviously dramatized. **Infantile** subtypes are the more hysterical of the other subtypes. They display extreme emotional outburst, are very demanding and clingy, and are very overbearing. **Vivacious** personality subtypes are very bubbly and carefree, seemingly types who often can be aloof or uncaring. **Disingenuous** subtypes are the darker side of Histrionic Personality Disorder. They usually are known for being scheming and double-crossing people, the slick one, so to say.

People who suffer from Histrionic Disorder need to be the center of attention, noticed, are overly exerted into every situation and conversation, and are sometimes difficult to deal with. Some of the symptoms can be difficult to deal with from the outside. Often you are unable to show genuine emotion with Histrionic

Personality Disorder, or your normal social behaviors skew how you actually express emotion. This can deter others from wanting to interact with you because they cannot trust what you are showing them at face value. There is also an increased chance of relationship issues and issues with same-sex friends. Many people who have this use their sexuality to gain the attention and praise they are looking for. This leads to a higher risk of being unfaithful or for causing disruption in friendships and relationships. There is a domineering lack of trust of someone who has Histrionic Personality Disorder, just as there is a lack of authenticity from someone who suffers from it.

When it comes to therapies for Histrionic Personality Disorder, there is really no true course of action. The only two ways the disorder can be somewhat managed is through medication and psychotherapy. Due to the attention-seeking nature of the disorder, group therapy and support groups is not a good idea. As for traditional psychotherapy, there can be some of the same issues due to the manipulative tendencies, false emotion, and over-emotion caused by the disorder. Medication, though, can be used to treat underlying issues such as anxiety, depression, hyperactive disorders, and behavioral issues that can be a foundation for intensifying the symptoms of Histrionic Personality Disorder.

When it comes to finding a way to escape and deal with Histrionic Personality Disorder, the best choice is self-exploration. Meditation is a vital relaxation technique and one that does not require the person to put on any false self or force any emotions. The idea is to go within yourself, explore who you are, how you really feel, what you need and want in life outside of the social productions. By using this technique, you are able to understand more about who you really are at the center of it all and thus put your social self in the spotlight for you to better understand or even disassemble.

As with many disorders that require an audience or a set attention rate, there is difficulty getting away from the addiction. The addiction is real; there is a need for this person to feel a certain way around people. Their inability to deal with conditions that put them in a less important position or a more vulnerable state is something they cannot easily deal with. Finding a way to cope without being so over-emotional or being an emotional put-off is the goal of someone wanting to no longer be burdened by the stigma of such an exuberant personality.

The 6 Subtypes of Histrionic Personality Disorder

Appeasing

This subtype is somewhat contradictive to many of the other symptoms of Histrionic Personality Disorder. These subtypes will go out of their way to help other people. They tend to be over-accommodating, easily manipulated, have very low will power, and will concede to most things that are asked of them. The excessive force and willingness is what can make this issue severe. Whether the attention-seeking aspect of the disorder is what drives them to be so overeager or they want to be seen as a victim always being utilized, the pliability of this subtype is easily seen as being over the top and not a normal reaction.[2]

Tempestuous

The tempestuous subtype is easily described as being a bit of an emotional mess. They are often moody, pouty, and at an emotional turmoil. At other times they can have very passionate and stormy mood swings, especially since they are easily angered or upset over minor issues. The brooding factor is what plays into the attention-seeking aspects. For the most part, the extreme areas of anger, sadness, or any other dark emotional state are very disconcerting to others. With these subtypes, you have the person who stands in the back, glaring or moping. They still receive the attention they want, and sometimes you can even pass it off as an aura of mystery, but for the most part they are an emotional conundrum for others. Since there is not a usual direct reason or occurrence to cause the constant brooding state or outburst, it is difficult to understand how to approach these subtypes.[2]

Theatrical

If you suffer from this subtype of Histrionic Personality Disorder, you often will struggle with knowing who you really are or how you would normally react. Most of your life is falsified to try to always put on the best or most wanted look or posture to obtain a specific reaction. They will always seem to be posed or have mechanical movements that do not match the way they actually feel. There is an obviously synthetic aspect to much of their look, speech, dress, and overall behavior. Sufferers come off as fake or dramatized, which they normally are. The actions become so ingrained, as they consistently make these dramatized and rehearsed behavioral responses.[2]

Infantile

This personality subtype is the opposite of the tempestuous in that the overly emotional aspect is more child-like. They are often very excitable, overly enthusiastic, extremely clingy, demanding, and overall very immature in their emotional responses. They will tend to seem almost hysteric at many points. Usually their laughter is too loud or prolonged, they tend to display overreactions, and they make a spectacle of themselves majority of the time. This is most especially seen in young teenage females. Though it is a call for attention, it is part of a much deeper issue of feeling insecure about themselves. Eventually the hysterics become very detrimental to how others perceive them and thus causing them more problems.[2]

Vivacious

Vivacious subtypes have some of the more minor symptoms of Histrionic Personality Disorder. Though their enthusiasm is often still a little over zealous, they have down periods and can often be seen as simply free-spirited. There is an undertone of narcissism as they will often scold others or brush off other people's emotions and push their idea of a more care-free, bubbly outlook. Another downfall to this subtype is their ability to seem flippant or uncaring at times. This reflects poorly on them, but is not actually any kind of personal affront. By not allowing other, and mostly negative, emotions to bring down their own feelings (despite the possibility of them being superficial), they are able to maintain a more upbeat attitude on the surface.[2]

Disingenuous

Disingenuous subtypes of Histrionic Personality Disorder are a step below the tempestuous in their moods. Whereas a tempestuous subtype would be trying to gain attention through their emotional and moody demeanor, someone with disingenuous personality issues would have a much darker undertone to push away the attention. They are often considered more mischievous and underhanded. They create their own antisocial persona by purposefully taking a more villainous role. They are seen as cheaters, scammers, double-crossers, and any other deceitful title that can be applied. Many of their actions are governed by their inability to really understand and accept the emotional reactions of other people. They do not quite get the idea of feelings and seem unaffected by any emotional outpouring. With this hindrance, it is very easy for them to do things that could benefit them but hurt or upset someone else. They can even be referred to as conniving, crafty, calculating, and plotting because any time they are not actively manipulating people, they are trying to think of how they can change a situation to best suit their own needs.[2]

What Causes Histrionic Personality Disorder?

Thus far, science is still undetermined as to the possible causes of Histrionic Personality Disorder. There are three possible theories. The first relates to the possible genetic and hereditary connections that can be linked to other mental disorders. There is also the possibility of a social connection with the early developmental environment that the patient has grown up in. The third theory focuses on the psychological and coping mechanisms created that may result in Histrionic Personality Disorder. Normally the disorder has an early adult onset and is not seen until the person reaches their late teens or early twenties.[1]

Genetically speaking, there is no scientific way to confirm that Histrionic Personality Disorder is in fact passed on. What can be seen is some of the underlying disorders that may cause or enhance this issue. There is also the fact of the familial relations having the same order and giving credence to the possibility that it has a genetic connection. Some other disorders can be linked. Usually there is a family history of anxiety, depression, hyperactivity disorders, narcissism, and other emotionally based conditions. These conditions, separately, do not mean so much in connection with Histrionic Personality Disorder; however, taken together, they present a possibility that there is a higher likelihood of hereditary disposition.

During childhood, there are situations that can manipulate a child's behaviors and lead to Histrionic Personality Disorder later on in life. For children that are spoiled or given an unnecessary amount of attention, they will tend to live with the expectation of consistently receiving such level of attention. Children that are able to get away with emotional outbursts, temper tantrums, and other displays of extreme emotions will have a tendency to continue this behavior later in life as well. Displays of this caliber in the early years are enabled, oftentimes unconsciously, by the people around the child. Though the disorder in itself does not truly manifest until late teens and early adulthood, it can be present in younger years simply as a tested behavior flourishing. Allowing such demeanors will then make room for the child to grow up continuing such attention-getting behaviors. By being allowed to get away with the behavior at a young age, the child grows up believing that the behavior is widely accepted and sees no need to change. Being that Histrionic Personality Disorder has a tendency to create the illusion of being a rewarding persona; the behavior will only continue and eventually get worse.

The third possible cause is a behavior created in order to help the child deal with certain situations. Using extreme behavior as a coping mechanism is completely normal. When the behavior is accepted and continued and used later in greater length, the problem becomes more apparent. Often, recognizing these displays as something used to cover for a darker history is key to helping someone cope with the problems. There is usually a deeper reason when what is being displayed are forms of Histrionic Personality Disorder in which one is defensive, shady, moody, morose, or in any way gaining attention by trying to be focally anti-social.

The 9 Most Common Symptoms of Histrionic Personality Disorder

1. Uncomfortable and/or Unhappy if Not Center of Attention

Being the center of attention is very important to them and a major symptom of the disorder in itself. When they are not the focus of a crowd, they feel lost in the crowd or unimportant to the people around them. That craving for the spotlight is somewhat of an addiction and a way for them to be able to accept social situations. In their eyes, it is to be in the middle of it all or not part of it at all. The need derives from the uncomfortable feelings they get when they are not able to receive a certain level of attention. The anxiety and stress, and sometimes even anger, can make the feelings intolerable. This increases their force of feigned emotions and extreme reactions around the people they are seeking attention from. Being that someone with Histrionic Personality Disorder has difficulties with emotions, the lack of attention putting them into an emotional state is very disconcerting to them. In this way, their behavior, regardless of inappropriateness, is their way of dealing with the emotions they do feel and do not understand.[1]

2. Displays Provocative Behavior for Attention

This can become a very serious problem in their own relationships, and can affect the relationships of their friends as well. Many same-sex friends will feel their relationship threatened due to the overt sexuality of the person with the disorder. Such person will also not hesitate to show sexual provocation towards a friend's significant other, simply because they see themselves as more attractive and sexual. They do not see it as being rude or cruel to the friend, they only see it as using what they have to be the most of something in other people's eyes. This is doubly difficult when they have a significant other themselves. Often the partner of someone with Histrionic Personality Disorder will be plagued with jealousy or infidelity issues because of such sexual displays.[1]

3. Emotional Expressions Do Not Seem Authentic

They can seem to flip from one extreme emotion to another. They can have a sad face at something you said and then jump to an overexcited look at the mention of something else. Many of these expressions come off as not being realistic for other people to acknowledge. With the quick change in emotional state, it is apparent that the person is not feeling a genuine response on the same emotional level. This is not only frustrating for others, but can be disconcerting as many people expect universal reactions to be acknowledged and not just bypassed in a quick moment.[1]

4. Utilizes Physical Appearance for Attention

Histrionic Personality Disorder will often dress up to stand out. The most usual style is one of a provocative nature. Females will often wear cleavage-showing tops and/or short skirts in order to gain more attention. They will also use more makeup. Both genders will pay closer attention to their vanity, overall. Hair is usually styled a certain way, clothes specifically picked out to look a certain way. Even if the style is made to stand out with a more negative connotation, like the darker looks or gang-like styles, they are still aimed at receiving attention.[1]

5. Speech Patterns are Impressionistic and Lack Authenticity

Many things they say are made in offhanded or nonchalant ways that make most of their comments seem either rude or that they are replying to something they see as insignificant. They will often use quotes, common expressions, or other lines that do not seem to have an authenticity to them. There is also a genuine lack of emotion about their speech patterns. As they are not normally feeling the emotion that is supposed to be expressed, the words seem to fall flat or be dull when heard. It is not a direct insult, but to many can come off as not caring.[1]

6. Express Themselves Dramatically and Theatrically

Histrionic Personality Disorder, there is a lack of real emotion, but an abundance of overly dramatized emotion. You see them use hand motions, bounce around or gesture when speaking, or do some other overly stressed movement. They will also use props or specific facial expressions to accentuate their points. Whether it is picking their nails with a knife while they put on a tough front, or exaggerated eye rolls and hand flaps to show disinterest, they find ways to add to their attention-grabbing moments.[1]

7. Easily Influenced in Order to Maintain Attention on Them

Though it may seem like this personality type is more of the one doing the suggesting, when faced with someone or a group of people that they are trying to get attention from, they are very easily influenced to do whatever is asked or suggested. They often go with the flow or will easily comply with doing bets and dares. They will tend to do whatever it takes to gain and maintain the most attention from others.[1]

8. See Relationships as Deeper and More Intimate Then They Actually Are

The majority of the public and social life of someone with Histrionic Personality Disorder is an exaggeration. This also applies to what they claim in their personal lives. Friendships are stronger, people they know are more interesting, and their relationships always have a deeper intimacy and significance than what they actually have. You will often hear them describe situations and feelings as being deeper or more than they actually are. In this way, they can hurt the relationship as well. By not being as emotionally involved as they say they are, it reinforces the lie of the relationship for them. Just because they tell someone they are in love or that their partner truly loves them does not mean that these feelings are really present or even that strong.[1]

9. Difficulty with Maintaining Same-Sex Friendships

Due to their overt sexual nature, they tend to push this onto anyone they perceive as a possible sexual interaction. With friends that have partners, this can be very problematic. In wanting the attention of their friend's partner and in order to reinforce their attraction to the other, they will push their sexuality onto the partner. This can even include outright and obvious flirting or even verbally stating their sexual interest. The uncomfortable atmosphere is enhanced due to the patient's inability to recognize and understand the awkward feelings of their friend and that friend's partner. This can lead to a disturbance in the friendship or even the possibility of damage to the friend's relationship. Even if the sexual pretenses do not necessarily cause any reactions, the continued forced interaction is enough to begin degrading the friendship as it is.

Common Therapy Methods for Histrionic Personality Disorder

1. Medication

Medication cannot be used for the disorder directly, but can be utilized in underlying conditions. Hyperactive disorders, depression and anxiety can all be managed by medication. Using a pharmaceutical route is not always good for everyone, and should be well thought of before deciding to take such a course of action. Medication comes with its own set of side effects and can sometimes be worse than the issue being treated. There is also a high risk of abuse with many of the medications used to treat hyperactivity, depression and anxiety. Histrionic Personality Disorder is a condition that can easily lead to substance abuse, and so giving such medications to people with high probability of abuse can be extremely dangerous.

The use of medication should be discussed with a physician. The symptoms that need medical control, and thus a prescription, will have to be gauged in order to see if the severity warrants medical interaction. Once the condition is isolated and the extent of the problem is decided, then the medication can be chosen. The type of medication and dose is prescribed depending on other medical conditions, health concerns, and likelihood of abuse.

Antidepressants and anti-anxiety medication can have either the same or complete opposite reactions. One of the high risks with this medication category is the side effects. Some can cause physical issues, but the most common problem is with the mental side effects. Many of these prescriptions, especially if prescribed inaccurately, can lead to a worsening of depression and anxiety, or even lead to the person becoming suicidal. Often when someone is prescribed anti-anxiety or antidepressants, they are also prescribed psychotherapy as well. This way a professional is able to monitor and keep track of how the medication is affecting the patient.

Some of the stronger anti-anxiety and antidepressant medications, and medications for hyperactivity disorders, are at an extremely high risk of being abused and used in a more recreational sense. There are high level medications that are more like tranquilizers, made to shut down over-emotional responses and backlashes. There are also medications that can be utilized to achieve a high or euphoria, and even in suicidal attempts. Hyperactivity medications have a history of being used recreationally and often cause more harm than good.

Regardless of what medication is given and how it is used, there still needs to be both physical and mental monitoring of the patient. Healing and overcoming issues cannot be done properly if the medical professionals do not know how their treatments are helping or hindering the patient. It is imperative to notify them when anything seems wrong or not what is expected from the medication. It is also important for doctors to make sure any medication prescribed is completely disclosed to the patient, including side effects, pre-existing conditions, possible interactions with other medications, and what the expected outcome is when utilizing the medication.

2. Psychotherapy

Therapy is usually the choice for any personality disorder. The exception for Histrionic Personality Disorder is group therapies. Unlike many other behavioral disorders, group therapy or support groups, even relationship therapy, can be detrimental to the process. The biggest factor is being the center of attention. In a group setting, you are able to easily acquire the attention you are always seeking. When the focus is primarily on the person suffering from the disorder, progress is hardly going to be made. This means the best route is one-on-one session with a professional psychologist or psychiatrist.

In a psychotherapy session, the goal will be to find if there is a root cause for the disorder and to help the person learn to utilize other outlets to deal with the conflicts of their personality and emotions. Even if an underlying issue is not found, there is still the ability to flush out what the person is really craving for. Though attention is an obvious answer, it is a vague and broad one. What needs to be discovered is what the person specifically seeks from people. Are they looking for acceptance, respect, fear, or another form of reaction? What they are seeking for helps discern why they are seeking it. Someone who purposefully wants people to be fearful or submissive to them is probably someone who has had a history in which submission and fear was used to control them. If they were looking for everyone to feel dependent on them, to the point of letting themselves be consistently burdened by others' requests and their compliance, then there is a history of some form of abuse, although in some cases, it is the opposite. Instead of abuse, the person could have had a spoiled childhood and they seek to receive pity and support from others by making themselves constantly available to assist people with anything while also making a big deal of what they do for these people. Histrionic Personality Disorder has many stems and each can branch into something much deeper or be as simple as a spoiled child seeking the same treatment as an adult.

Once in a session, the therapist will have to be very observant of the interactions they have with the patient. Being that the exaggeration of emotions, history, and personality are to be expected, hidden clues will be much more necessary to find out more about the person's actual disposition. Paying attention to falsetto tones, emotional responses that do not affect the facial muscles and eyes, and other small cognitive motions that give away deception would be very useful. With Histrionic Personality Disorder, there is another layer of therapy occurring while the person is participating in simple talk therapy. The therapist must utilize their keen observations, deductions, and understanding of human perception and mental processes in order to truly understand the patient. Though the patient may be saying or doing one thing, it is up to the therapist to interpret what they are really dealing with. It will take some time for enough trust, and for the idea of a new audience, to wear off enough for the patient to be able to truly confide in the therapist. The achievement of this can be quite successful as long as the therapist maintains neutrality when dealing with the patient's eccentricities.

How to Overcome Histrionic Personality Disorder

Histrionic Personality Disorder is not something that can easily be overcome. In fact, it is more of something in which balance must be sought and maintained in order to cope with the problems. If you are trying to help someone with Histrionic Personality Disorder, the most challenging aspect is helping the person realize that how they interact with the world is harmful to them and the people around them. Once they have realized this issue, then you must address the specific ways that they are not completely integrating themselves in a socially accepted manner. From there, you can then find a way to redirect the attention needs in ways that are healthier and more beneficial. Finally, there needs to be help from those that are closest to the patient, and thus usually those that are more often hurt by them.

What someone believes about themselves is a focal point that is very difficult to change. Perceptions of our own successes, failures, and how we think others see and think about us are usually pretty unmoving ideas pegged in our minds. The most difficult task is done in our heads, through our own thoughts. In order to deal with the need and addiction of consistent attention, you must find other outlets to satisfy the need that are more conducive to social acceptance. People-watching, without the interaction, can be very helpful. Watching others interact, how they approach people, talk to them, how their relationships unfold and progress, and any other aspect of human functionality can give a first person understanding of what people are comfortable with and what is the best way to approach people.

Relationships with a significant other and with close friends are the most likely to be harmed with Histrionic Personality Disorder. A crucial area that needs the most attention in your life is with the person you are closest to. Especially since most people that try to have a functioning relationship with someone that has this level of emotional and attention-centered need is very difficult to deal with. If someone has been able to handle the pressures thus far, it is safe to say that such person deserves a change that makes them the center of your life, rather than you the center of your life. Self-centered behavior can negatively impact a relationship as it is. Once the attributes of overly sexualizing yourself, constantly seeking sexual attention elsewhere, and over dramatizing your relationship, have begun to impact the relationship, it is up to you to fix this. The first step is to regain focus on your partner. Excitement of new sexual interactions is often the leading cause of straying from the relationship. With this in mind, inserting new things into your own relationship and changing old routines can help in recreating some of the excitement. It is also important to realize that most people fall into a stagnation after a period of time. It is up to both of you to maintain the relationship and that means that you have to make changes as well as accept certain aspects. Understand that what you do to seek attention harms your partner, and if you genuinely love and respect this person, especially if they have tolerated your habits this long, they deserve your efforts.

As with intimate relationships, familial relationships can also be negatively impacted by your social interactions. If you are prone to making spectacles at gatherings, being cruel or rude to others, or even overly extending yourself in order to be the victim, you must acknowledge and change the behavior. Again, observation of how your family interacts is a first step. Seeing how people mingle, socialize, and interact in groups and one-on-one will give you an idea of what you are lacking in these settings. Learn to pull back; do not always try so hard to be in the center of things. Learn to not be so vocal or self-centered in discussions. Ask how other people are doing. Even if you are not interested or have a hard time finding an emotional connection, the act of inquiring is enough for some people to feel better about you and how you respond to them. Although it does not help with the falsification of emotions, sometimes feigning emotions on a lower level can do great things for others. You have to learn not to overdo the emotion though. Know that putting on exaggerated facial expressions, being loud about your responses, or inadvertently redirecting your attention while you are talking with them is detrimental to the process. Level with the person, watch them. You can even make a mental game to help keep yourself preoccupied. Look for stress lines in their face, how they use their eyes, what hand motions they do. Most of these indicators can give you a good insight into how they are feeling and what response they are looking for.

Friends, especially same-sex friends, are often another aspect of your life that needs your attention. With same-sex friends, the biggest conflict lies in your interjection of their love life. Many times there is an odd sexual tension built up, especially if the friend's significant other is in your company at times. Using your sexuality for the attention of the people that are loved by those closest to you is a very harmful thing to do. You have to learn to treat their partner as another friend or as an extension of them. Once again, this is a person that has probably dealt with your habits and attention-seeking behavior on many occasions. They are used to your attitude and emotional outburst and may even be used to your inappropriate reactions to their partner. They deserve your efforts as well. Again, pull back and be more observant. Watch them for emotional keys and indicators. Do not overlay your own needs over them. Misinterpreting their reactions to suit your wants and needs is the downfall of these situations. You need to realize they need attention too. They also need your support and your ability to be a part of their lives without causing conflicts in their lives. It is critical that you make minor changes and adjustments especially around their partners.

Because of your need for attention, so much is focused on you, on your thoughts and behavior. Although how someone with Histrionic Personality Disorder behaves is very negative, this does not make you a bad person. This makes you someone who has learned a way of doing things that may seem the most efficient, but is not the most effective. A lot of people need the comfort of knowing that you can reciprocate attention and focus and that you can be there for them as much as they have been there for you. If you find yourself losing friends, unable to maintain relationships, and failing in social settings, it may be time to reevaluate how you are dealing with these moments of interactions. If you can, find out what is bothering them, what exactly you do that hurts them. Blatant honesty can be painful and hurtful, especially when it conflicts with the narcissistic and delusional aspects of this personality type. No one wants to hear that they are self-centered, rude, conniving, or attention-seeking. Realizing that you come off as desperate and insecure is a crushing blow to the ego. This can even lead to a rebound in which more attention is sought through self-woe. Try, instead, to be open and honest. Tell people what goes through your mind, why you feel this way, why you do what you do to get attention. Communication is very important. Once people understand that you have a mentality that makes you seek attention in these ways, they may have better ways of helping you cope as well as helping you get what you need without you causing so much damage to them and their own mental states.

How to Find Your Escape

As with many other personality disorders, the one thing you truly must escape from is your own mind and thoughts. The first step is to be away from people. People give you the attention you need and therefore feed the problem. The second step is finding outlets that are safe but effective for you. Many will turn to harmful behavior and addictions to fill any voids. You have to find an escape that suits you, gives you the relief you need without harming your health or mental state. Being open to alternative ideas can also help. Look into meditation. There are many forms of meditation and many ways to help you escape your mind for short or long periods of time, in a healthy way that allows you to get more in touch with your true feelings and emotions.

The first concern with escaping yourself in any manner is the use of substances to achieve such escape. Though this can temporarily achieve the desired effect, it is harmful in the long run and even in its initial use. One of the biggest movements currently is the use of marijuana in medicinal as well as recreational capacity. Though many states have not completely legalized the substance, it is a growing trend. Being conscious of the laws in your area and maybe even having a medical professional give their opinions on the subject, the utilization of marijuana should be considered wisely. When used responsibly, it has the ability to allow a person to relax, curb any underlying anxieties, and can also benefit in meditation and any activity that seems too slow or static. Prescription medications can also benefit in helping anxiety and hyperactivity but they must be used in the way they are prescribed to prevent adverse effects. Nevertheless, the use of any substance should be regulated. Even if it is an occasional alcoholic beverage to help curb the stresses and restlessness, it is easy to fall into a habit of abuse.

Meditation is a common suggestion but one which is not usually followed. What many people do not realize is how easy it is to use. Meditation can take anywhere from a few minutes to several days. Anything more than an hour or so is something utilized by gurus of the lifestyle and not something suggested for someone needing an occasional break. Once you get down the basics and understand the benefits first hand, then you can begin longer sessions if you feel so inclined. The biggest thing you are trying to do is to shut out outside noise, worries, and stimuli. One of the simplest techniques is to visualize a "happy place." Trying to just empty your mind and focus on nothing is a near impossible task, especially with a mind that is overactive or constantly focused on the outside world. Make a mental scene or place that seems peaceful to you. Some like a river or stream in the woods, some like beaches, some picture themselves fishing or doing another calming activity; it all depends on your idea of a peaceful scene devoid of other people. Picture the scene in your head, with eyes closed in a comfortable environment that you are not likely to be disturbed in. Slowly bring your other senses in. The first is visual, pay attention to details. Visualize the reflections of light, the small details around your scene. Add in the sounds you would hear in this place, what is expected in such an environment. Then try to focus on smells of the grass or the air and the feel of the breeze or sun. As you add your senses into the scene, you will be able to slip deeper into the scenario. Going to this place for even a moment can help you reflect in a situation where you need calm. As you get more confident and more used to going to your happy place, then you can begin to try to use self-reflection. Think about you and about the things that make you happy and what drives you. As you meditate more and use the time to understand yourself more, you will be able to get a more level look on things around you.

Conclusion

Histrionic Personality Disorder is difficult to understand for those around the person as well as the person themselves. The need for constant attention, and the process the person uses to get that attention, can be a challenge for everyone involved. Realizing the foundation of the habits, the primary habits that make up the person's disorder and overcoming the issues involved is a daunting process. There are several forms of the disorder, subtypes that focus on specific ways the person seeks out the attention they need. Once a problem has been identified, specified, understood, and accepted, there are steps to take to try to make life easier on the patient and the people closest to them. As the biggest negative effects of this disorder are cast on the people near the person with the disorder, it is important for them almost more than the sufferer to find a way to cope. Utilization of medication and other alternative forms can be put into play to try to help focus more on the main problem. The biggest changes, though, must come from and in the mind and way of thinking of the person who suffers from the disorder.

Subtypes are ways to categorize the manifestation of specific symptoms that result from the overall disorder. Appeasing subtypes will go overboard trying to help or assist others in order to achieve a victim status. They will constantly be at the beck and call of people and will go out of their way to do things for others only to later complain about how they are being used in order to gain the sympathy of people around them. Vivacious personality types are overly bubbly, seemingly unaffected by other people's emotions or difficulties, and give off a carefree type of persona. Tempestuous subtypes put off a moody and dark disposition. They use their negative aura to keep people at bay but at the same time, use the "dark and mysterious" persona to gain attention. Disingenuous subtypes are the shady and underhanded people. They trick and scam their own friends and like the attention they receive for being this dangerous person. Theatrical people are overly exaggerated in every aspect of their behavioral displays. Their speech is synthetic, their clothing is made to catch attention, emotions are brief and overdone, and they usually come off as being entirely fictitious in their outward appearance. Infantile personalities are the ones that come off as childish and highly insecure. They will throw actual tantrums, tend to be very clingy, and exhibit exaggerated emotional outbursts.

Symptoms cover a wide range of attention-seeking behavior and reasoning. The primary symptom is a necessary level of attention in order to make them comfortable. They have a tendency to display inappropriate sexualized behavior. Their emotions are constantly changing and seem to be less than authentic to other people. There is a focus on their physical appearance and style to constantly stand out or fit a certain preconceived notion. Their speech patterns are usually practiced and do not seem to reflect the person's actual disposition. Their emotions are over the top and overly exaggerated and expressed. They are easily influenced by the people around them in order to constantly be in conformity. When referring to actual relationships they are in, they will make them out to be better, more intimate, and less factual than they actually are. Relationships with same-sex friends are often damaged by their overly sexualized behavior to the opposite sex, most of whom are their friend's' partners.

Science has yet to determine a true cause for this personality disorder. There are many theories as to what could be the dominant cause. Though genetics is a separate possibility, it relies on the presence of other disorders and mental conditions being present to account for it being the main condition. The majority of cases are people with childhoods or environments that constructed these habits as a coping mechanism or a way to gain attention. They expect a certain level of attention from everyone and pushing in any way to gain that level leads to the extreme nature of Histrionic Personality Disorder. Although the disorder is not usually seen and diagnosed until the late teen years or early adulthood, it is something that can be present as a possibility earlier in life. In this case, it is easier to trace the source and use such factors to overcome the disorder later in life.

Treatment of Histrionic Personality Disorder consists of medication and psychotherapy. Medication used to treat depression, anxiety, and/or hyperactivity disorders can lower the effect of the disorder and allow for a lessening of the overall symptoms. The big problem with the medication approach is that there is a high risk for the abuse of the medicine. Medication also comes with the down side of having side effects that can be counterproductive to helping overcome the disorder. Psychotherapy is the most likely way to seek outside help. With one-on-one sessions, the therapist has a chance to try and see how the person reacts without an audience. The difficult aspect to psychotherapy is that a lot of pressure is put on the therapist to try and figure out the true nature of the person's actual feelings and behaviors.

If you have Histrionic Personality Disorder, learning to overcome it is a matter of understanding your own thought processes in social situations versus the way other people think and react. Most of the challenge lies within your own head and changing how you actually think. There are often issues with a lack of empathy and inability to deal with down time of any type. With this hindering you, and on top of practiced behavior, it can be difficult to change your approach, much less your mind. Focus must be made on watching and learning from the people around you. Often you are so used to focusing on your own acceptance of others and the attention you receive that you do not lend much credence to how other people are tolerating your actions. Although being capable of empathy is a biological and physiological factor, being able to learn how to seem more empathetic is a matter of time and focus spent learning, and using what you have learned to replicate the behaviors. Toning down the theatrics and being less prone to begging for attention through aggravation and pettiness is another process that needs to be learned.

Escaping yourself and the thought patterns that make you act the way you do, is a matter of personal ability. Many people turn to the use of drugs and alcohol to escape. This is dangerous to you and the people around you. Many substances can enhance your behavior and make things worse. Others can have side effects that can lead to fatal outcomes. Marijuana is a current substance being used and petitioned for all over the

United States. It is important to understand the laws in your area and to abide by them. It is also crucial to know exactly what it is, what it does, and how it can impact you. The use of this compound can be effective in helping someone calm themselves, lowering the hysterics, overemotional reactions, and exaggerations. Another useful technique is meditation. Meditation does not take as much skill and focus as someone may think would be required. Many meditation techniques can be done in a matter of minutes and does not require candles and incense and music. Although you can learn to use mediation on a higher scale, just taking a few moments from the world to give yourself a brief time of reflection or relaxation will go a long way to help soothe the frustrations.

Histrionic Personality Disorder is a complicated issue to deal with. Persons who find themselves dealing with the problem usually do not see that there is a problem. Changing the very way others think and act is a very hard task to do. Incidentally, changing one's own thinking patterns and how that is manifested in their actions is even harder. If you are someone with Histrionic Personality Disorder, it takes a lot for you to see these problems and to make any changes to how you are in social situations. The very basis of your behaviors is the attention you receive. It is more likely that you will use the fact that it is a disorder to gain more attention than to see it as a need for change. You have to realize that the spiral can eventually lead to a total absence of any attention. People are only tolerable of unacceptable behavior for so long before they eventually tire of it. This is even truer when it comes to romantic and/or intimate relationships and close friends. Although those people may have a higher tolerance and do care for you enough to put up with a certain extent of attention-seeking, they will eventually have to abandon you in order to be able to function in other social circles. With same-sex friends, your actions can harm their own relationships with other people and leave them no choice but to no longer interact with you. You have to find a way to cope without the constant attention. Once you are able to realize the problem and the need for a change, you can then take the journey and steps to better yourself for your own good.

Final Word/About the Author

I was born and raised in Norwalk, Connecticut. Growing up, I could often be found spending afternoons reading in the local public library about management techniques and leadership styles, along with overall outlooks towards life. It was from spending those afternoons reading about how others have led productive lives that I was inspired to start studying patterns of human behavior and self-improvement. Usually I write works around sports to learn more about influential athletes in the hopes that from my writing, you the reader can walk away inspired to put in an equal if not greater amount of hard work and perseverance to pursue your goals. However, I began writing about psychology topics such as Histrionic Personality Disorder so that I could help others better understand why they act and think the way they do and how to build on their strengths while also identifying their weaknesses. If you enjoyed

Histrionic Personality Disorder: The Ultimate Guide to Symptoms, Treatment and Prevention please leave a review! Also, you can read more of my general works on *How to Get Out of the Friend Zone, Avoidant Personality Disorder, Sundown Syndrome, ISTJs, ISFJs, ISFPs, INTJs, INFPs, ESFPs, ESFJs, ESTJs, ENFPs, ENFJs, How to be Witty, How to be Likeable, How to be Creative, Bargain Shopping, Productivity Hacks, Morning Meditation, Becoming a Father,* and *33 Life Lessons: Success Principles, Career Advice & Habits of Successful People* in the Kindle Store.

Like what you read?

I write because I love sharing personal development information on topics like why people behave the way they do with fantastic readers like you. My readers inspire me to write more so please do not hesitate to let me know what you thought by leaving a review! If you love books on life, basketball, or productivity, check out my website at claytongeoffreys.com to join my exclusive list where I let you know about my latest books. Aside from being the first to hear about my latest releases, you can also download a free copy of *33 Life Lessons: Success Principles, Career Advice & Habits of Successful People*. See you there!

Endnotes

[1] "Histrionic Personality Disorder Symptoms." *Psych Central.* Web. <http://psychcentral.com/disorders/histrionic-personality-disorder-symptoms/>.

[2] Millon, Theodore, Ph.D., D.Sc. "Personality Subtypes." *Personality Subtypes Summary.* Web. <http://www.millon.net/taxonomy/summary.htm>.

Made in the USA
San Bernardino, CA
06 November 2015